THE GIGAWIT DICTIONARY OF THE E-NGLISH LANGUAGE

COMPILED BY
TONY HENDRA

EDITION 1.0

Copyright © 2000 by Tony Hendra

All rights reserved
Printed in the United States of America
First Edition
ISBN 0-9702455-0-5

The text of this book is composed in Adobe Bembo.
Composition by Tom Ernst, Hilary Barberie.
Manufacturing by The Ace Group.
Book design by Brian Collins.

| Join us at gigawit.com |

preface

preface (n.)*:* 1. pompous preamble to mind-glazingly dull work, whose grandiosity varies inversely with the worth or interest of ensuing content; 2. falsely modest disclaimer of responsibility for brilliance of ensuing content in favor of those who, while unable to ensure a book's success, can certainly guarantee its failure, as for example: "editors" "publishers", vice-presidents in charge of "promotion" and other talent-free lunch-munchers; 3. insincere expressions of thanks to friends, spouses or circles of professional acquaintance, without which an author can be certain of patronizing, irritable, or scandal-mongering reviews in small, incestuous literary journals, social ostracism up to and including exclusion from weekends in the Hamptons and extended loss of connubial rights; 4. insincere expressions of thanks to nit-pickingly anal "copy-editors", slack-jawed "fact-checkers" and incalculably ignorant "line-editors", whose closest experience of literary style has been chopping cocaine at a Vassar homecoming party with the torn-off cover of *The Sun Also Rises*; and who have been convinced by their anti-canonical academic mentors that their own creative talents are as valuable and unique as that of Dante, Jane Austen, William Faulkner, Eudora Welty,

Julian Barnes or the author whose work they are currently butchering; 5. portion of a published work so seldom read that it presents the opportunity for an author to reveal for the first time in any public forum that a certain top executive of a certain New York publishing house with an ampersand in its name, likes to be spanked by a cut 'n buffed Filipino fellow wearing only flip-flops and an eye-patch.

I would also like to thank my children, Toots and Tosh, my mother Viveca Sackville-Sissinghurst and of course, the ever-faithful Freckles, my mongrel muse; without them this book would never have seen the light of day. God bless you all and get jiggy with it.

Tony Hendra
New York City
May 2000.

P.S. Join us at gigawit.com

THE
GIGAWIT DICTIONARY
OF THE
E-NGLISH
LANGUAGE

COMPILED BY
TONY HENDRA

EDITION 1.0

a

algorithm: technique of deep hypnosis enabling Al Gore Jr. to clap along at R&B concerts.

alt-energy: actually knowing what the Alt key does and having the flat-out gosh-darn courage to use it.

@: the syllable a-t as in 'the c@ s@ on the m@' or 'The c@ sh@ on the m@' Less often with proper names: 'C@hy s@ on M@t' '@tila the Hun had bad @titude' 'Linda Ronst@ is un@tractively f@' Occ. used with long 'a' sounds as in 'Bill G@tes should buy @ &T'.

agriculture: terrifying pre-analog system out in the boonies somewhere with obscure connection to microwave technology.

 1. puny phallic symbol relentlessly thrusting upwards to its goal, falling back only to push back up, up, up, never down, never limp, always rigid, always ready for more; 2. Any way you look at it a mouse penis.

AI (Artificial Intelligence)*:* George W. Bush.

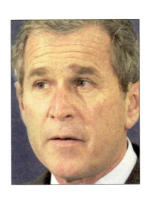

AI
(Artificial Intelligence)

analog world: 1. miners digging coal from holes with picks made of steel from ore other miners dig from other holes and send to coal-fired steel smelters to make more picks; 2. roughnecks drilling oil to fill trucks with fuel for assembly-lines where workers build pick-ups roughnecks need to drive to the rigs to drill more oil. 3. just a total nightmare.

ARPANET: interlocking system of computers developed by the U.S. military during the Vietnam war to let all ranks from grunt to four-star general air their hopes, fears and dreams, exchange information about everything from pets to peeves to recipes, and deliver consumer items at competitive cost directly to his or her barracks. In short a FUN Phil-Silvers kinda military where everybody could get along in a safer, friendlier world.

art: data arranged in really weird configurations, sometimes in frames.

atom: analog-era particle of matter, once considered the basic building block of the Universe; now being replaced (according to e-theorists like Nicholas Negroponte) by the bit, a web-era particle of data. An example of Negroponte's Principle: the recent disappearance of Mount Rainier.

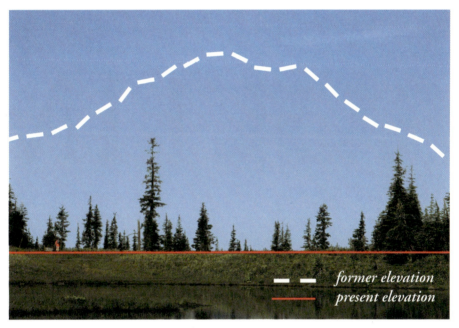

Mount Rainier (former)

world's largest old-new-media
conglomerate:

AOLTIM

Martha

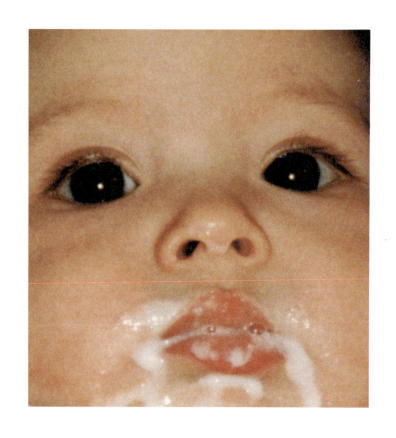

\ *(back-slash):* warning motion given by a venture capitalist before he actually stabs you in the back.

baby: the ultimate in wetware.

bandwidth: The aggregate lateral width during performance of a rock band and their equipment.

bandwidth bottleneck: too many rock bands of too great an aggregate lateral width trying to get onstage at the same time.

Bertelsmann: third largest media conglomerate in the world and only publisher with its own on-line bookstore which first came to prominence under the Nazis, allegedly providing the Wehrmacht and the SS with countless millions of copies of reading material. Current owner of the largest trade publisher in the U.S., Random Haus.

banner ad: annoying, garish, roiling frieze, usually in the top third of a screen, which can only be removed by clicking through it to someplace you don't want to be, selling something you don't want to buy.

Berners-Lee, Tim: inventor of the Internet, but still, by all accounts, a nice guy.

biotech: biology is *so* destiny.

binary digits: two fingers entwined; often symbolizing hope for success in an uncertain enterprise or outright misrepresentation, such as an Internet IPO.

bit: small metal tool-bar which revolutionized human civilization by turning the horse into a navigable search engine.

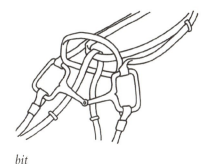

bit

binary code: computer system which reduces all data in the Universe to two symbols: an erect, upright stick and a round, inviting hole.

blah-blah-blah: common reaction of cyboors when their utopian vision of the tech-intensive future is questioned. (cf. *YAWN! Get-used-to-it*)

bot: creepy, crawling agent thingy that sniffs around for stuff you might like. A lot like any other agent.

bottom bounce: 1. movement of a stock rebounding from a low; 2. degree of bounce or vertical jiggle in a bottom. (Usually fem. but see Cambridge University Treasury of Unseemly Verse, 1938):

> *There was a young chorister of Kings*
> *Whose mind dwelt on heavenly things*
> *But his secret desire*
> *Was a boy in the choir*
> *With a bottom like jelly on springs.*

Bignum: incredibly stupid troll overlord dropped at the last minute from *The Lord of the Rings*.

breathlessness: hyperventilation; universal quality of all e-journalism.

broadband: rock band with unusually large bandwidth e.g. ZZ Top, The Weather Girls.

buzz: onomatopoeic term denoting intense activity by certain species of insect.

Bignum

BTR: 'Break the Rules'; common sentiment of Internet manifestos; suggesting that committed users question every commonly accepted belief except the following:

I
THE INTERNET IS
THE GREATEST BOON
TO HUMANKIND
SINCE SMOKED CHEESE

II
ALL RECORDED
HISTORY
LED UP TO MP3

III
ONE PLUS ONE
EQUALS ELEVEN

CEO: Chief Expletive Officer

change agent: one who has made, or is about to make, a nice piece of change.

charity: the act of giving away tens of billions of dollars over a number of years, secure in the knowledge that you will earn back twice as much during the same period.

click-'n-drag: a transvestite approaching in high heels.

cocaine: highly addictive drug that a. costs significant sums of money in incrementally larger amounts; b. causes users to babble incoherently for hours to other users often about either embarrassingly personal matters, or the profoundly spiritual nature of the drug experience itself; c. causes users to lose all track of time, particularly between the hours of 8 PM and 8 AM.

clicks-and-mortar: consumers who research purchasing options on-line, shop in a bricks-and-mortar retail outlet and are in possession of desired items within 3-5 hours. (Still available for e-journalism coinage: Bics-and-mortar, hicks-and-mortar, kicks-and-mortar, licks-and-mortar, Knicks-and-mortar, micks-and-mortar, lipsticks-and-mortar, pricks-and-mortar.)

CFO: Corporate Flying Object

CIO: Chief Impotence Officer

code: 1. sequences of numbers or symbols used to obfuscate routine messages and designed to be understood only by operatives with special or secret missions.

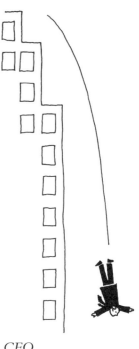

CFO
(Corporate Flying Object)

Content: Typing.

Clark, Jim: super, *super* guy we're hoping will back our IPO.

conditional: standard tense of e-journalism as in 'could assemble atoms in appropriate formations to make gold' (cf. implied conditional of common e-j usages: *'still needs to position itself'*, *'it remains to be seen if consumers will* ——', *'the answer lies in the future'*, *'we're in Day 1 Week 1'*, *'still in the toddler stage but just wait for puberty'*)

convergence: 1. process by which all screen-related media forms: television, the Internet, motion pictures, security cameras will converge to a single screen; 2. gathering of unusually dunce-like providers to type content for same.

Mr. Jim Clark!

C++: Jennifer Gates' grade average.

contractor: 1. (antiq.) one who undertakes to employ workers to fulfil a contract; 2. (mod.) A worker without a contract.

cool: 1.(antiq.) belonging to a cultural subset whose intellectual and artistic attitudes are in advance of the majority's; 2. (mod.) pertaining to any commodity which a commercial enterprise wishes to sell to the majority, whether it be cheese-puffs, snuff-porn, SS Waffen shoulder-flashes, edible underwear or Republicans.

cyboor: an Internitwit, an Internut, an e-jerk, an IPOaf.

cookie: small furry animal which follows you home and which you'll learn to wuv just as much as it wuvs you.

cookie

crash: Not now
FOR CHRISSSAKE!!!
I'VE GOT A
PRESENTATION
IN TEN
MIN

cyberspace: 1. (as per William Gibson's *Neuromancer*): "lines of light ranged in the non-space of the mind, clusters and constellations of data. Like city lights receding..."; 2. (as per computer activist John P. Barlow): "that place you are in when you're talking on the telephone"; 3. communication medium which combines all the thrills of pen-palling with the intense excitement of ham radio; 4. bottomless self-loathing experienced by staying up all night scribbling notes to total strangers whose lives are so impoverished that they stay up all night scribbling notes to total strangers; 5. vast hollow tree crammed with overweight Lost Boys looking for a Wendy; 6. sluggish, heavily polluted virtual sub-atmosphere which makes every communicative task slower, clumsier and hugely more expensive than it need be; 7. the Tower of Banal; 8. oblivion into which millions of jobs will one day disappear without a trace; 9. winner in mid-90s 'cliche-race' over alternative candidate 'fiberspace'.

data: limitless reservoir of fascinating information available to web-users, such as: a. the role of formic acid in the manufacture of textiles; b. what the weather was in Winnipeg on the morning of March 3rd 1953; c. the veterinary term for the inside wall of a goat's colon.

database: the stage of unclothing which can be achieved on a date.

Allowable stages of unclothing recognized by the International Convention on Human Dates (ICHD). Adopted Geneva January 15, 2000.

data-glove: hot, sweaty, smelly, wearable control-unit allowing user to approximate in a small room experiences he's too chicken to have on a hang-glider, rock-face, race-car or Harrier jump-jet.

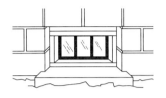

daughter window

daughter window: small aperture in basement wall allowing a female child to return home without the knowledge of a parent, after having sex in the back of '83 Camaro.

datom: speculative particle comprising half data, half matter, that may be basic building block of the universe.

day-trader: a fool, a gull, a sucker.

dead-tree book: content presented in a compact, portable form, varying in size between a Palm Pilot and a laptop, which requires no booting or Internet connection but whose owner must act as search engine; and whose provider is usually compensated.

denial of service: not tonight hon, I gotta headache.

death: 1. removable gene in human DNA; hence 2. (Calif.) an option; 3. frequent impediment to e-topian projections concerning life extension; 4. Frequent result of unforeseen tech-evolutions for example smart rooms which can reconfigure themselves on a Hannibal Lecter template.

defenestration: 1. to throw Bill Gates out a window.

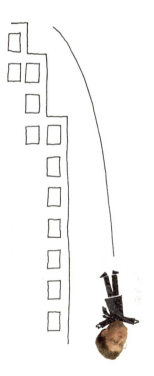

defenestration

digital: pertaining to, or operated by, or explored by, or excited by, a finger.

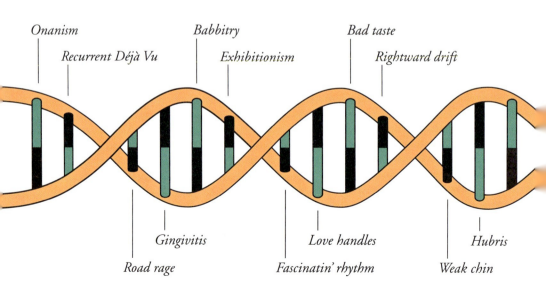

Onanism
Recurrent Déjà Vu
Babbitry
Exhibitionism
Bad taste
Rightward drift
Gingivitis
Road rage
Love handles
Fascinatin' rhythm
Hubris
Weak chin

digital divide: gap between computer-haves and have-nots which makes it impossible to sell the poor goods on-line, collect intimate details of their private lives or offer them instant sexual auto-gratification. Soon to be eradicated by federal legislation providing them with a 'safety Internet.' (cf. *'web-fare bums' 'web-fare queens'*)

DIS: what DOS will become after Disney Inc. buys Microsoft.

DNA: data in jelly; (from Brit. Data-iN-Aspic) (cf. *Fr. data en gelée*): destiny, fate, kismet, jug ears, bad skin, big bones, genetic predisposition to those lumpy wart things Dad had growing all over his face.

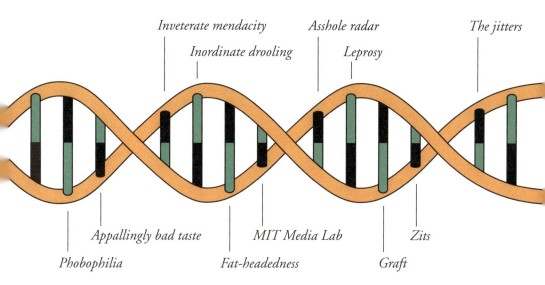

dot-com:

common misspelling of the term

dot-con

dotted quad

dotted quad: traditional English dessert made from beef suet and fermented gooseberries; (cf. *'spotted dick'*)

domain: 1. (old Fr.) properties of monarch, duke, lord or other aristocrat, usually lands which have been in one family for many centuries; 2. (mod. Fr.) vineyards, particularly in Burgundy, producing wine of outstanding quality; 3. (U.S.) 40 acres of cyberspace and a mule.

down-load: to acquire the money of another by issuing grossly inflated stock in a company that has no assets or prospect of profit. Hence ***down-loaded':*** 1. to be less drunk than you were the night of your IPO; 2. to be less insanely wealthy than you were last week. (cf. *'networthless'*)

down-stream server: uniformed employee of catered fishing trips in the Pacific North-west who work downstream from the anglers (i.e. in the direction they move, typically having responsibiity for the sit-down courses including wine service. (cf. *'upstream-server'*)

dystopia: any proposed alternative to e-topia.

drop-'n-drag: military term for ordering a soldier to do push-ups in woman's clothing.

drop-'n-drag

 *e-:* prefix denoting variously, 'electronic', 'exciting', 'exceptional', 'ethereal' or 'echh!' which just about e-veryone in the e-nglish-speaking world is so sick to death of, they're ready to e-gurgitate.

*e*lect
*e*coli
*e*jaculate
*e*motion
*e*rupt
*e*eeeech
*e*quality
*e*go
*e*cology
*e*lectric chair
*e*ternal
*e*vil
*e*maciate

*e*nough, *e*ready.

early stage specialist: a frequently unemployed person.

edi (electronic data interchange)*:* revolutionary technology costing a few paltry millions, which allows business-to-business transactions to be conducted on-line instead of on paper and which for some goddam reason these stupid smaller companies refuse to goddam install.

eight digits: 1. golden handcuffs; 2. Afghan Internet user who has been reprimanded by the Taliban. (cf. *Khyberspace*)

e-liberalism: digitally remastered version of Kennedy-era progressivism which concentrates on comfort levels rather than MEGO Big Ideas, as in: 'OK, OK, so the Texas State Penal System is an international human rights outrage. At least our restaurants are smoke-free'.

e-net: 'Internet' pronounced by a Londoner who lives east of St. Paul's Cathedral.

e-male: chronically under- or over-weight person of masculine gender, with bad skin and a burning need to type.

e-mail: any sentiments, commands, concepts, reflections, opinions, of sufficient incoherence and banality that they would never have been expressed before the digital means to do so became available.

end user: you, babe.

engineer: highly paid employee of Internet-based companies whose only role is to act as a lightning rod for the rage, frustration and fatigue of all other employees.

e-vil: bad code in the wet-ware, dude.

eyeball: scanning device attached to a willingness to waste time and money.

extranet: additional device for restraining unruly hair or catching shrimp.

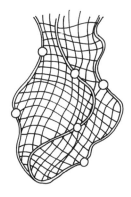

net

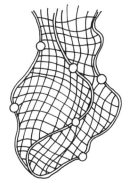

extranet

f

fiber-space: squishy term (derived from 'fiber-optics') denoting parallel universe created by AI; beaten out in mid-90s 'space'-race by the now familiar 'cyberspace'.

firewall: electronic block to outside access, so named to make it sound as substantial as an actual firewall made of bricks and mortar, instead of some insubstantial slabs of code, which is all it is, let's face it Charlie.

flamebait: object of intense desire who happens to be underage. (Not applicable in South Carolina, Louisiana, Alabama.)

fish 'n chips: cold-blooded aquatic life-form implanted with micro-electrical mechanical systems.

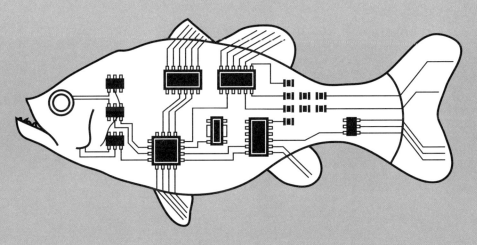

fish 'n chips

freedom: ideal of individual liberty generally held to have been much expanded by cybernetics, a discipline developed by the military-intellectual complex to a. better communicate and prevail in a nuclear holocaust and b. establish unquestioned authoritarian control of surviving sectors.

fat media: media for fat people.

frictionlessness: a lack of traction or abrasion between two interfacing surfaces, much sought after in e-commerce but disastrous while driving or having sex.

fast: not one hundredth as much fun in any important human activity (e.g. eating, sex), as S

                          S

                                  L

                                       O

                                       O

                                              W

                                           W

                                              W

                                                W W W

g

G-surf: to ride the interior wall of a breaking wave wearing only a G-string.

g-spot: highly sensitive, pinkish-red protuberance in the dead center of a Thinkpad, which controls its .

get it: to get it, you know? Either you do or you don't you know? If you don't, what's the point? FOAD.

golden handcuffs: resting till you vest.

go root: to plunge deeper than ever before, to return to the innermost core, to feel the earth move.

God: (see code.)

Gutenberg: silly old Kraut who invented moveable type.

Gutenberg, Johannes

hacker: 1.(antiq.): hero, pioneer, free spirit, 2. (mod.) sociopath, saboteur, criminal.

hand: symbol denoting the 'invisible hand' of the e-market, or the Law of Demand and No Supply, which holds that stock-value rises in direct proportion to the lack of goods and services supplied.

hard drive: Dakar to Khartoum. Six thousand klicks of pure unpaved hell.*

*(cf. *Ulaan Baatar to Volgograd, that's a bitch too*)

The Law of Demand and No Supply

Stock-value rises in direct proportion to the lack of goods and services supplied

help: mega-menu of non-existent Windows functions which trigger sub-menus of non-existent Windows solutions to problems encountered when non-existent Windows functions malfunction, none of which includes how to Stop Print.

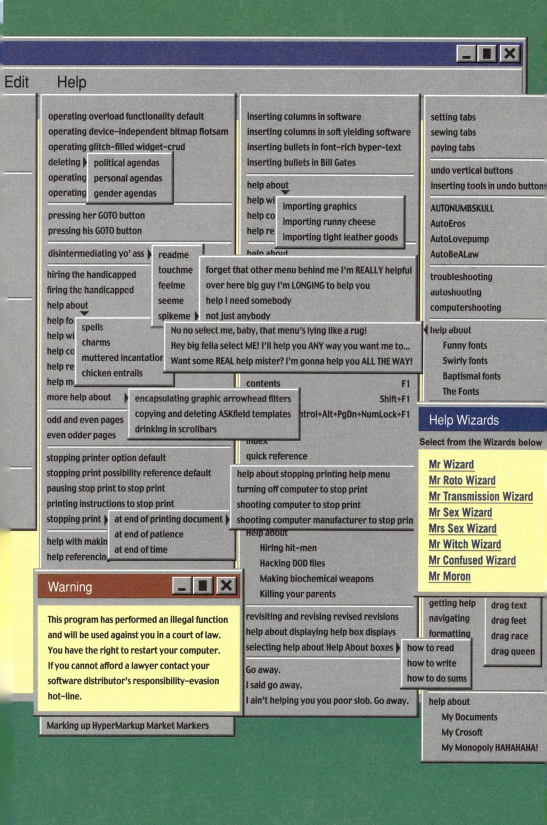

hard, wired: Martha Stewart.

Hi-Res Retina Display: amazing new technology which beams TV directly into the eyeballs making it impossible to mute or click off commercials.

hip: halfway between hype and hope.

Head Start 2: government program once proposed by President Clinton as a destination on the Information Superhighway, making federally funded oral sex available to all.

Hitler: 1. World War 2 German leader without whose crimes against humanity no chat-room discussion could ever be conducted; 2. Name of British Royal Family before it was changed to Windsor.

history: important events which preceded in time-space, what we refer to as 'now'. Significant examples: Faraday's discovery (1813) of electricity, Luigi Malatesta's discovery (1879) of the takeout pizza, Leibniz' discovery of something to write with.

 immemorial symbol denoting the ineffably sad, sweet, glorious and inglorious finity of life.

*Her Majesty
Queen Elizabeth II*

human genome: small humanoid often portrayed in medieval doublet with pointed cowl; regarded in legend as inferior to, and occasionally slaves of, dwarves. (cf. *the genomes of Zurich*)

hyperlink: a link. (cf. *superdupergigaterajumbocolossallink*)

IPO (Initial Pubic Offering): to expose yourself publicly in the hope of being paid a fortune.

illegal operation: any useful, simple, speedy operation which software manufacturers have omitted from their program or do not wish you to perform.

INS: 1. (Intentional Naming System): advanced computer software capable of deciphering your innermost desires and fulfilling them; 2. (Immigration and Naturalization Service): federal agency capable of deporting you if you do.

intellectual capital: pervasive oxymoron (cf. *'military intelligence' 'postal service' etc.*)

Information Superhighway

Internet (Intern-et): a young female intern.

Information Superhighway: cracked and crumbling, weed-clogged federal infrastructure project, abandoned by the White House after 1996 Presidential election.

InterWeb: what the Internet will become before it evolves into a worldwide network of compulsorily worn sweater-like computers called the Interknit.

Intern-et

j

jacked-in: 80s term for interconnectivity, frequently used by jack-offs.

Java applets: small inedible fruit grown in Java.

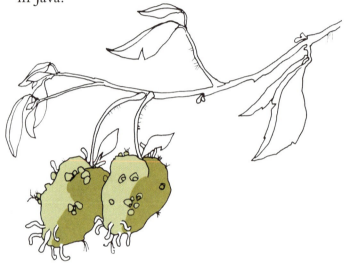

java applets

Justice Department: obscure federal agency which has proposed splitting Microsoft into two companies: a really, really *small* company called Micro; and a really, really *nice* company called Soft.

Khyberspace: that part of cyberspace occupied by the Taliban. *(Warning: use of digital technology in Afghanistan is punished by removal of two or more digits. Use of a manual is punished by removal of whole hand.)*

Kleiner, Perkins, Caufield and Byers: Satan.

kid: occasional by-product of sexual interface entirely motivated by conviction that all things are possible and that whatever he or she fantasizes, should immediately be made available. (cf. *MIT Media Lab*)

killer app: to make a sudden loud appearance behind Strom Thurmond.

Kleiner, Perkins, Caufield and Byers

1

laptop: that which may sit on or 'atop' one's lap; first used by the 'inventor President' Thomas Jefferson to describe his companion Sally Hemings.

life extension: revolutionary genetic engineering which will extend to 200 years or more the amount of time humans spend in a nightmarishly surveilled and controlled tech-intensive world.

logarithm: 'I'm a lumberjack and I don't care...' (cf. *Spam*)

Luddite: one who hates tech-heads and vice versa.

mall: marketplace where buyers meet sellers face to face, make a transaction and leave with, respectively, merchandise and money.

Mars Lander: advanced mobile computer system designed to land on and reconnoiter the surface of the planet Mars; shot down Sept. 19th 1999 by the Martian Tactical Air Defense Force.

mafia.com: 'dese, 'dem and DOS.

me-mail: e-mail for egomaniacs.

m-commerce (alt. sp. 'McCommerce', Alistair)*:* famous Scottish bagpiper (1887-1956) known for his powerful drone.

Martha Stewart: prominent macro-bot.

masturbation: common male activity on which the only genuinely profitable sector of the Internet is based.

matrix: female supervisor, usually clad in studded, black-leather corset and knee-length spike-heel boots, employed in British boarding schools to discipline pupils.

menu bar: a bar which serves no food or drink but offers a number of toothsome and nutritious menus.

microbots: micro-chip-sized mobile sensors built on a crab-like insect-template with exoskeleton and six legs. *(Warning: if you find one in your underwear it is a federal crime to squish it.)*

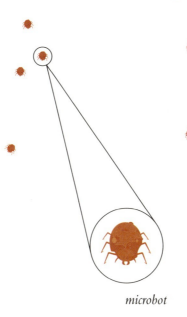

microbot

MIT Media Lab: lavishly funded research program dedicated to the principle that if something can be thought of, it should be brought into being.

moby (colloq.)*:* the largest (usually applied to the male pudendum).

model: 1. flawless fantasy object holding out promise of limitless fulfillment at relatively low cost; 2. woman or man who wears sample clothes to promote their sale.

Moore's Law: principle of cyber-physics which holds that on-line consumption of chips will double your weight every 18 months.

mouse: wee, timorous, plastic beastie now head-to-head with Mickey for world domination. (cf. *The Holy Rodent, Holy Rodent Empire*)

MUD: ground floor of the Tower of London.

multi-task: to perform three or more types of work at the same time, all of them atrociously.

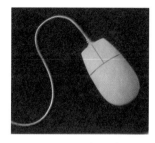

wee, timorous, plastic beastie

MP3: second half of Einstein's famous equation:

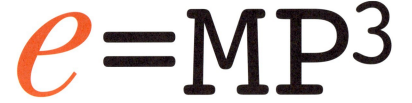

navigate: to intuit simultaneously all the variables of sea, wind, current, hull–dynamics, displacement and sail-area, while scudding across the sun-speckled swells of a turquoise ocean, the salt-sea spume cooling your brow, to who knows what paradises of surf and sand and sybaritic sex; 2. sitting in a darkened room clutching an oval chunk of plastic.

net: 1. (abbrev. 'Internet'; *as per* Dr. Johnson's Dictionary: 'net: a series of holes held together by string'): a series of interstitial communication strings held together by hot air. Hence 2. ***net play:*** a series of holes held together by venture capital; 3. profits; outmoded fiscal term denoting the amount remaining when operating expenses are deducted from gross receipts.

netwit: one who fancies himself a web-humorist and all-round funny typist; much devoted to Wall Street question-jokes, emoticons and talk-mode acronyms like HHHHHHHHOK.

Nic Handles: Rochester Redwings AAA shortstop of the early 50s, with legendary ability to pick off line-drives.

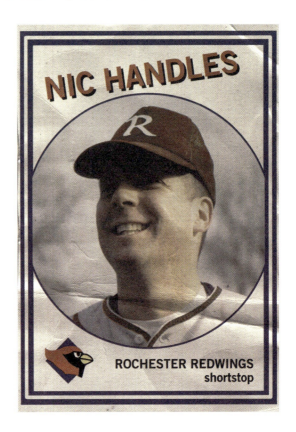

TABLE OF COMMON NETWIT ACRONYMS

PHAIOYUCTYS: Please hold an item of your underwear close to your screen.

CIHAMOYT?IHMWSAINTFTGBTJ: Can I have a moment of your time? I had my wallet stolen and I need three fifty to get back to Jersey.

IGTAUTDSVSIWUTPUYMAAALIGOBDI4PJTOOKNKIOSMOC!: I'm going to ask you to do something very special I want you to pick up your mouse and lick it go on baby do it for Poppa just this once OK now kiss it O MOTHER OF CHRIST!

WITPOMA: Where is the pen of my aunt?

GOAD: Gurgle off and die!

JOAD: Jack off and die!

ROAD: Rut off and die!

TOAD: Totter off and die!

WOAD: Waddle off and die!

CRUDY: Christ aren't you dead yet?

obesity: (alt. sp., *e-besity*): life-threatening, visually repellent condition affecting more than 50% of all Americans, commonly arising from a. not rising from a sitting position to do your shopping on foot in a mall or market; b. not rising from a sitting position to go to a public place and communicate with other humans; c. not rising from a sitting position to perform services for your employer; d. not rising from a sitting position to have sex; e. not rising from a sitting position ever, except to browse the fridge or accept a UPS package.

on-line: 1. (antiq.) waiting for service; 2. (mod.) still waiting. (cf. *28.8 kbps*) *omniscience:* all-knowingness; quality once attributed to God, Allah, Siva, Zeus and Manitou. Now available to any Web-user for pennies a day.

Office Assistant: 1. Cartoon of William Gates Jr. in the shape of a paper-clip that appears without warning on the bottom right-hand corner of Microsoft Word offering useless assistance in elementary tasks; 2. Human employee with advanced knowledge of abstruse computer commands who can actually remove the damn thing from your software.

Office Asssistant

organ-farming: custom among Mennonite farmers of carrying a small harmonium in the cab of their combine-harvester.

outsource: 1. (corp.) to hire another company to perform services you are incapable of, or too incompetent to perform; 2. (pers.) to hire another to perform services you are too busy underwriting dot-coms to perform, such as having your annual physical.

out-the-door: accelerated schedule allowing a dot-com to go on-line and begin charging for its service, but only after every aspect of its program including ethical concerns, technical glitches, hyper-links etc. have been scrupulously re-examined, finalized and coordinated. (cf. *fix-it-later, floating point error*)

off-line: the real world, countryside, birds, flowers and stuff.

packet-sniffer: dog used by the DEA to detect substances in the bodily orifices of drug couriers. Hence *packet-sniffing:* common psychopathic disorder of FedEx employees.

PalmPilot: handheld computer whose tiny keyboard thankfully makes typing stream-of-consciousness e-mail all but impossible.

pizza: staple food of web-users consisting of data-grain and data-vegetables topped with data-cheese made from the data-milk of data-cows.

perception: 1. (antiq.) antonym for reality; 2. (mod.) synonym for reality.

ping: quantum of euphoria experienced by an animated Disney character.

pixel: quantum of fairy-dust sufficient to induce a ping.

JUST TWO LOST BITS IN CYBERSPACE!!!

privacy: outmoded notion that intimate personal information about an individual is the property of that individual, when in fact it's the property of FATAL ERROR FATAL ERROR ERROR FATAL ERROR FATAL ERROR FATAL ERROR

FATAL ERROR FATAL ERROR FATAL ERROR FATAL ERROR FATAL ERROR FATAL
FATAL ERROR FATAL ERROR FATAL ERROR FATAL ERROR FATAL ERROR FATAL
FATAL ERROR FATAL ERROR FATAL ERROR FATAL ERROR FATAL ERROR FATAL
FATAL ERROR FATAL ERROR FATAL ERROR FATAL ERROR FATAL ERROR FATAL
FATAL ERROR FATAL ERROR FATAL ERROR FATAL ERROR FATAL ERROR FATAL
FATAL ERROR FATAL ERROR FATAL ERROR FATAL ERROR FATAL ERROR FATAL
FATAL ERROR FATAL ERROR FATAL ERROR FATAL ERROR FATAL ERROR FATAL
FATAL ERROR FATAL ERROR FATAL ERROR FATAL ERROR FATAL ERROR FATAL
FATAL ERROR FATAL ERROR FATAL ERROR FATAL ERROR FATAL ERROR FATAL
FATAL ERROR FATAL ERROR FATAL ERROR FATAL ERROR FATAL ERROR FATAL
FATAL ERROR FATAL ERROR FATAL ERROR FATAL ERROR FATAL ERROR FATAL
FATAL ERROR FATAL ERROR FATAL ERROR FATAL ERROR FATAL ERROR FATAL
FATAL ERROR FATAL ERROR FATAL ERROR FATAL ERROR FATAL ERROR FATAL
FATAL ERROR FATAL ERROR FATAL ERROR FATAL ERROR FATAL ERROR FATAL
FATAL ERROR FATAL ERROR FATAL ERROR FATAL ERROR FATAL ERROR FATAL
FATAL ERROR FATAL ERROR FATAL ERROR FATAL ERROR FATAL ERROR FATAL
FATAL ERROR FATAL ERROR FATAL ERROR FATAL ERROR FATAL ERROR FATAL
FATAL ERROR FATAL ERROR FATAL ERROR FATAL ERROR FATAL ERROR FATAL
FATAL ERROR FATAL ERROR FATAL ERROR FATAL ERROR FATAL ERROR FATAL
FATAL ERROR FATAL ERROR FATAL ERROR FATAL ERROR FATAL ERROR FATAL
FATAL ERROR FATAL ERROR FATAL ERROR FATAL ERROR FATAL ERROR FATAL
FATAL ERROR FATAL ERROR FATAL ERROR FATAL ERROR FATAL ERROR FATAL
FATAL ERROR FATAL ERROR FATAL ERROR FATAL ERROR FATAL ERROR FATAL
FATAL ERROR FATAL ERROR FATAL ERROR FATAL ERROR FATAL ERROR FATAL
FATAL ERROR FATAL ERROR FATAL ERROR FATAL ERROR FATAL ERROR FATAL
FATAL ERROR FATAL ERROR FATAL ERROR FATAL ERROR FATAL ERROR FATAL
FATAL ERROR FATAL ERROR FATAL ERROR FATAL ERROR FATAL ERROR FATAL
FATAL ERROR FATAL ERROR FATAL ERROR FATAL ERROR FATAL ERROR FATAL
FATAL ERROR FATAL ERROR FATAL ERROR FATAL ERROR FATAL ERROR FATAL
FATAL ERROR FATAL ERROR FATAL ERROR FATAL ERROR FATAL ERROR FATAL

Pringles

PDA (Personal Digital Assistant)*:* one whose services are in some way related to the finger: e.g. a manicurist, a proctologist.

Pringles: communion wafer of the One True Faith of Universal Connectedness.

philanthropy: addressing financially the social injustices and inequalities which made you rich enough to address them.

portal: hole, door, opening, aperture, orifice, through which data or matter may pass. Hence (colloq.) *'Fred, don't be such a flaming portal.'*

paper: flat, white fiber bills come on.

RAM: Random Access Mammary. Illegal in most states.

Redmond, Wa.: Wa. to you too.

repeat visits: common symptom of inflamed prostate.

replicator: large-fanged reptile that reproduces itself endlessly.

rich media: media owned and operated by the rich.

Romatherapy: behavior modification technique used in Italian penal system; recalcitrant prisoners are subjected to odors distilled from the alleys of the Trastevere.

replicator

scriptorium: large chamber in medieval monasteries in which monks copied by hand important Church documents; earliest known form of Kinko's.

Selectric: still got one stashed someplace? Hold on to that sucker.

semi-conductor: 1. any substance through which electricity passes inefficiently: e.g. wet straw, pork; 2. one who leads an orchestra through only half a composition; 3. one of two persons who leads an orchestra through an entire composition; 4. leader of an orchestra with a day-job; 5. French driver of an American truck.

service economy: an economy consisting overwhelmingly of servants.

S

Selectric

server farms: plantations in which servants are raised at minimal cost.

Siamese twins: the ultimate in shareware.

silicon: good for memory, bad for mammary.

slacker: one who works 90-hour weeks with no union benefits, no collective bargaining, no prospects of advancement other than meaningless stock options and may be a tad pissed off about that.

SIS (Social Insecurity Service)*:* top-level proposal being developed by Microsoft for a new federal agency to address adverse effects of chronic long-term Web-abuse. Proposed divisions include the CIA (Central Impotence Agency), the FDA (Food and Diet Administration) the IRS (Individual Responsibility Service), SELF re-education loans (enabling re-habbed Web-abusers to learn Sanskrit, truffle-farming, the Origins of Glitter-Rock, BMW repair: any subject which will return them to the off-line world and meaningful self-absorption). Costliest proposal: Beautify America! which would provide federal funds for state-of-the-art fanny-tucks, jowl-elimination, thigh-resizing and abdominal liposuction to all recovering Web-addicts.

SOCIAL INSECURITY SERVICE

smart: 1. (room): a room that knows you're in it and how to stop you getting out; 2: (person): someone who wouldn't go near a smart room on a bet.

SPAM: unwanted communications. Derived from Monty Python's Flying Circus, a TV series considered cutting-edge 30 years ago. (cf. *Rosetto, Lou, love of early work of Bob Dylan; grok' (from '*Stranger in a Strange Land', 1966)*; 'freds and barnies';* other cutting-edge tech-usages)

spit bits: to beam messages of a suggestive nature from a Palm Pilot at attractive women in airports.

square: one who confines his or her entire experience of life and the cosmos to a pre-conceived grid, or rectangular screen.

squinters: tiny-lensed, wire-rimmed spectacles designed to make even the most boneheaded or rapacious CEO look studious, revolutionary and uninterested in material advancement.

stickiness: virtual bonding material which keeps an eyeball glued to a screen, but which must not impede frictionlessness.

Trotsky

Lenin

Ballmer

streaming media: media for people who keep their PC and TV in the same room, right next to the bed and the fridge.

suit: one who neither leads nor follows nor gets out of the way.

surf-at-work: common diversion of serfs at work.

SWS: Sudden Wealth Syndrome: overnight accretion of billions of dollars, pounds, deutschmarks etc., a condition which only Americans believe requires psychiatric treatment.

the-mail: analog mode of delivery involving the transportation of goods from point A to point B by public or private carriers, without which e-commerce would collapse in 3-5 days.

talk: that which used to be cheap, but now costs 20¢ a minute.

tech support: blue-collar workers required to perform menial tasks in white shirts.

teleport: fortified vintage wine of Oporto (Portugal) broken down into constituent data, e-mailed to recipient and reconstituted for his or her drinking pleasure. Any day now.

teleporting: technology which converts a person into data and sends him or her via optic cable at slightly less than the speed of light to St Louis. Currently stalled due to multiple head-on fatalities with person-data arriving *from* St Louis.

test-bed

test-bed: cot, couch or other location on which a VC assesses a prospective investee's level of readiness for a massive infusion of capital. (cf. *seed-stage*)

template: 1. a temporary plate (e.g. in the head); 2. a tardy secretary.

Things That Think: lavishly funded program at MIT's Media Lab posited on the insane notion that the vast majority of the world's population wants objects, appliances, dwellings or vehicles with a mind of their own. (cf. *Human Things With Their Hats on Backwards That Barely Function*)

Trekkie: one who is likely to purchase inordinate amounts of groceries from Priceline.com.

toolbar: Tim Allen's favorite watering-hole.

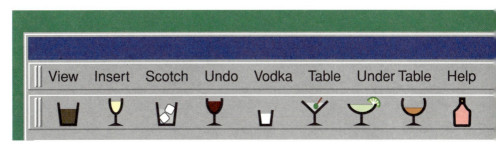

toolbar

upstream server: uniformed employee of catered fishing parties in the Pacific North-West, standing upstream of the anglers near the point where they start, typically with responsibility for aperitifs and passed hors d'oeuvres such as blini with caviar, stuffed mushrooms, mini crab-cakes etc. (cf. *downstream server*)

upstream server

uptime: length of time a penile erection can be maintained. Usually measured in minutes or seconds, but in some cultural subsets, hours.

Utopia: word coined by Sir Thomas More in 1514 in his eponymous satire; derived from the Greek 'ou' ('no') and topos ('place') hence 'no place' 'nowhere' 'a place that does not and cannot exist'.

URL: guy who operates Yahoo's server in Biloxi, Mississippi.

URL

VC: 1. (19th cent.) Victoria Cross: award for extraordinarily courageous and heroic actions against overwhelming odds; 2. (20th cent.) Viet Cong, adversary renowned for sneaky, duplicitous, backstabbing techniques of combat. Hence 3. (21st cent.) *Venture Capitalist:* EITHER a courageous hero who prevails against overwhelming odds OR a sneaky duplicitous, back-stabbing adversary.

virtual: close but no cigar; example: 'Jason decided to use virtual equipment to rappel down Bryce Canyon and broke his stupid neck.'

VPN (Virtual Private Network)*:* what an entertainment dot-com becomes if it has ample content but no subscribers.

valuation:

WHAT?????
YOU gotta be
KIDDING!!
NO? HAHAHAA
HAHAHAHAHAA
HAHAHAHAA!!
YOU MUST BE
FLEEPING
NUTS!!!!
THAT'S...

THAT'S... OHOHOH MY GENTLE JESUS! I'm LOSING IT! HEHEHHHHE- HEHEHEHHH- HAHAOH!!!!!!! GOD! Sorry.

Really.

wealth-creation: collective non-binding agreement by the wealthy that something is worth more than they had previously thought.

web: sticky polyhedral net enabling certain insects to ensnare biologically inferior victims and suck out their life-blood.

Webpage (L.I.)*:* small township adjacent to Bethpage L.I., whose inhabitants are often born with amphibious feet.

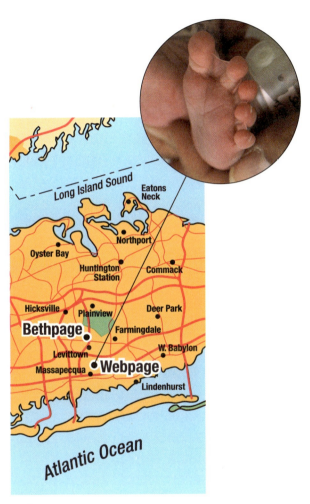

Webpage

wet-ware: term for human brain coined by those who believe that software created by the human brain can actually evolve into an cyber-brain superior to the 'wetware' that created it, which is just about the sillie FATAL ERROR
ERROR FATAL ERROR FATAL ERROR FATAL ERROR
ERROR FATAL ERROR FATAL ERROR FATAL ERROR
ERROR FATAL ERROR FATAL ERROR FATAL ERROR
ERROR FATAL ERROR FATAL ERROR FATAL ERROR
ERROR FATAL ERROR FATAL ERROR FATAL ERROR
ERROR FATAL ERROR FATAL ERROR FATAL ERROR
ERROR FATAL ERROR FATAL ERROR FATAL ERROR
ERROR FATAL ERROR FATAL ERROR FATAL ERROR
ERROR FATAL ERROR FATAL ERROR FATAL ERROR
ERROR FATAL ERROR FATAL ERROR FATAL ERROR
ERROR FATAL ERROR FATAL ERROR FATAL ERROR
ERROR FATAL ERROR FATAL ERROR FATAL ERROR
ERROR FATAL ERROR FATAL ERROR FATAL ERROR
ERROR FATAL ERROR FATAL ERROR FATAL ERROR
ERROR FATAL ERROR FATAL ERROR FATAL ERROR
ERROR FATAL ERROR FATAL ERROR FATAL ERROR
ERROR FATAL ERROR FATAL ERROR FATAL ERROR
ERROR FATAL ERROR FATAL ERROR FATAL ERROR
ERROR FATAL ERROR FATAL ERROR FATAL ERROR
ERROR FATAL ERROR FATAL ERROR FATAL ERROR
ERROR FATAL ERROR FATAL ERROR FATAL ERROR
ERROR FATAL ERROR FATAL ERROR FATAL ERROR
ERROR FATAL ERROR FATAL ERROR FATAL ERROR
ERROR FATAL ERROR FATAL ERROR FATAL ERROR
ERROR FATAL ERROR FATAL ERROR FATAL ERROR
ERROR FATAL ERROR FATAL ERROR FATAL ERROR
ERROR FATAL ERROR FATAL ERROR FATAL ERROR

FATAL ERROR FATAL ERROR FATAL ERROR FATAL ERROR FATAL ERROR FATAL
FATAL ERROR FATAL ERROR FATAL ERROR FATAL ERROR FATAL ERROR FATAL
FATAL ERROR FATAL ERROR FATAL ERROR FATAL ERROR FATAL ERROR FATAL
FATAL ERROR FATAL ERROR FATAL ERROR FATAL ERROR FATAL ERROR FATAL
FATAL ERROR FATAL ERROR FATAL ERROR FATAL ERROR FATAL ERROR FATAL
FATAL ERROR FATAL ERROR FATAL ERROR FATAL ERROR FATAL ERROR FATAL
FATAL ERROR FATAL ERROR FATAL ERROR FATAL ERROR FATAL ERROR FATAL
FATAL ERROR FATAL ERROR FATAL ERROR FATAL ERROR FATAL ERROR FATAL
FATAL ERROR FATAL ERROR FATAL ERROR FATAL ERROR FATAL ERROR FATAL
FATAL ERROR FATAL ERROR FATAL ERROR FATAL ERROR FATAL ERROR FATAL
FATAL ERROR FATAL ERROR FATAL ERROR FATAL ERROR FATAL ERROR FATAL
FATAL ERROR FATAL ERROR FATAL ERROR FATAL ERROR FATAL ERROR FATAL
FATAL ERROR FATAL ERROR FATAL ERROR FATAL ERROR FATAL ERROR FATAL
FATAL ERROR FATAL ERROR FATAL ERROR FATAL ERROR FATAL ERROR FATAL
FATAL ERROR FATAL ERROR FATAL ERROR FATAL ERROR FATAL ERROR FATAL
FATAL ERROR FATAL ERROR FATAL ERROR FATAL ERROR FATAL ERROR FATAL
FATAL ERROR FATAL ERROR FATAL ERROR FATAL ERROR FATAL ERROR FATAL
FATAL ERROR FATAL ERROR FATAL ERROR FATAL ERROR FATAL ERROR FATAL
FATAL ERROR FATAL ERROR FATAL ERROR FATAL ERROR FATAL ERROR FATAL
FATAL ERROR FATAL ERROR FATAL ERROR FATAL ERROR FATAL ERROR FATAL
FATAL ERROR FATAL ERROR FATAL ERROR FATAL ERROR FATAL ERROR FATAL
FATAL ERROR FATAL ERROR FATAL ERROR FATAL ERROR FATAL ERROR FATAL
FATAL ERROR FATAL ERROR FATAL ERROR FATAL ERROR FATAL ERROR FATAL
FATAL ERROR FATAL ERROR FATAL ERROR FATAL ERROR FATAL ERROR FATAL
FATAL ERROR FATAL ERROR FATAL ERROR FATAL ERROR FATAL ERROR FATAL
FATAL ERROR FATAL ERROR FATAL ERROR FATAL ERROR FATAL ERROR FATAL
FATAL ERROR FATAL ERROR FATAL ERROR FATAL ERROR FATAL ERROR FATAL
FATAL ERROR FATAL ERROR FATAL ERROR FATAL ERROR FATAL ERROR FATAL

wheel

wheel: pre-analog mode of transportation, which digital engineers reinvent several million times a week.

wired: state of irrational euphoria induced by illegal stimulants; commonly applied to the tertiary or 'cranky' stage.

Wired People Magazine: new magazine from AOLTimeMartha scheduled to appear in January 2001, providing inane gossip and inspiring fables about sullen e-celebrities with all-black wardrobes.

written to spec: useless, inoperable, worthless.

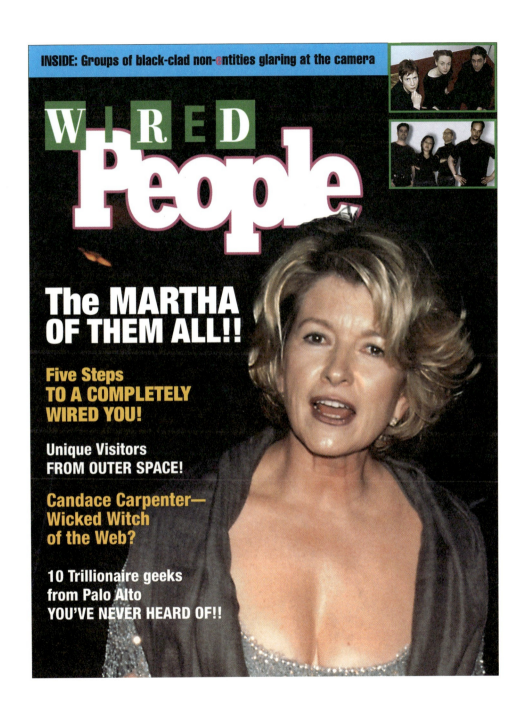

XML (Extra Medium Large): size of T-shirt worn by Paul Allen when dieting.

XXXL: rare growth chromosome which enables certain humans to sit motionless without sleep for weeks on end.

Y1K: significant date in history of Western Europe, which caused massive dislocation when monks had to learn to recognize dates in four digits. Y1K also caused heated debate within the Church over which animals and plants to illuminate the extra zero with. There were huge delays continent-wide: leeches lay uncollected in ditches, heretics scheduled for eye-gouging had weeks of extra vision.

Yeehaw!: what Yahoo! is called in the eleven states of the old Confederacy.

Y2.001K: estimated date Disney Inc. will take over Microsoft to form mega–corp Mickeysoft.